CW00538668

a pint
for the ghost

poetry

helen mort

tall-lighthouse

for Mum, Dad and Danny

Acknowledgements: I would like to thank Arts Council England for their generous support of this project and Writers' Centre Norwich for the mentoring they provided through the Escalator scheme. Huge thanks are also due to Aoife Mannix, Patrick Morris, James Grieve, Issam Kourbaj and Sam Genders for their role in the development of the script for live performance and special thanks to Tim Wells for M.R. James stories, pints and ghosts a'plenty.

Thanks also to the following friends for their support and advice: Iain Milner, Charmian Banner, Alan Buckley, Benjamin Morris, Tom Chivers, Ed Sharpe, Ian Cartland, Michael Bayley, numerous Derbyshire landlords and all the ghosts of the Peak District.

Thanks also to the editors of *Rising* and *Blackbox Manifold* where several of these poems first appeared.

the Norman MacCaig quotation is taken from the poem *Ancestry* from *The Poems of Norman MacCaig*

the John Burnside quotation is taken from the poem *The Good Neighbour* in the collection of the same name

the Robert Frost quotation is taken from the poem *Ghost House* from the collection *A Boy's Will*

cover image: *at the duke of edinburgh - lee*
l k robinson
cover photo: katie utting

published 2009
ISBN 978 1 904551 73 7
www.tall-lighthouse.co.uk

contents

*'The ghosts I never saw
and don't believe in
won't go away.'*

Norman MacCaig

Whenever I think about poetry, or the act of writing itself, I've always found myself coming back to the idea of ghosts: people and places we once knew, characters we've never met, stories we overhear and wish were ours. I'm fascinated by those ghosts and how a poem can reinvent them, encounter them in unlikely places; the way you can slip into a bar in a strange town and think you see an ex in the corner, nursing a whisky.

I was born in Sheffield and spent most of my years as a teenager in nearby Chesterfield, with its Crooked Spire and peculiar legends. Growing up in Derbyshire, I was always aware of what a singularly ghostly place it is, how many stories are attached to the landscape. In particular, I was interested in the ghosts of former industry; miners and steelworkers who haven't downed tools though the pits and foundries have shut. Sheffield is rife with ghosts, from the ancient sailors in The Ship Inn, to the Hillsborough spirit who pinches the black ball from all the pool tables in the pubs...

This collection developed from a desire to re-tell some of these local legends, and introduce a few ghosts of my own. The poems in *a pint for the ghost* were written for my performance piece of the same name; a show set in a shabby pub, after closing time, where ghosts arrive to introduce themselves. This pamphlet is a companion to the live show. The stories that form part of the performance are not included here, but can be accessed on the website *www.apintfortheghost.blogspot.com*, where you can also add your own ghost stories.

These are poems that invoke different characters: ghosts with unfinished business, ghosts who warn of danger, personal ghosts, even living ghosts. What all these spirits have in common is a reluctance to be put to rest. To reiterate Norman MacCaig - *even the ghosts we don't believe in won't go away*.

early doors

are you being served?

There are pubs
where the front door
shuts behind you
like a coffin lid

and strangers
throwing darts
stop their game
to stare you out.

Pubs still cast
in smoke so thick
you barely see your hand
before your face,

where the lights
stay dim, the floor unswept,
the glasses taste
of mushroom spores.

Silent pubs
where nothing moves
or breathes except
a small, white dog

who bares his teeth
until you slink away
out into the rain
you came from.

Pubs where the landlord
eyes your every move
and doesn't say a word,
or, worse, draws close

to read your fortune
in the dregs left
at the bottom of your glass,
talks of market days

and heavy weather,
meetings in the rain,
danger in the
cruel, bright frost.

Pubs you've seen
before in dreams,
down long, untravelled
country roads

or by the river
where you lost your way,
went stumbling through
the city's dark

and from your sleep
you've seen their lights,
you've heard them
call to you:

it's getting late -
won't you come in?
Won't you draw up your chair
and drink again?

passing strangers

'...cell by cell, a heartbeat at a time,
my one good neighbour sets himself aside
and alters into someone I have known:
a passing stranger on the road to grief
husband and father; rich man; poor man; thief'.

John Burnside

a pint for the true shepherds

Now the chance has gone, I wish
I'd bought that man a pint:
the farmer who sat silent next to me
through Midnight Mass, and raised
his eyebrows as the well-fed vicar
revelled in the story of the gentle shepherds
*(friends, how like The Lord's own servants
are the men round here who still
keep animals today)*. And as the organist
received the nod to play, the man
who hadn't spoken took his cue at last,
rose to his feet, said: *Reverend,
tha knows nowt about sheep.*

a tinny for mikey

Between the chip shop
and the strip club,
Mikey weathers Friday night,
his blanket draped
over his head, fingers
working on a roll-up
no-one else can see.
He lifts it with a steady hand
then licks the air
from left to right, places it
invisible between his lips,
waves me over to the doorway,
asks me if I have a light.
And when I shake my head
afraid I don't,
he grabs me by the wrist
and pulls me close,
and as he looks straight through me
whispers *don't be afraid*
of anything, darling.

a guinness for the sceptic

He loves a pint of Dublin's finest
for its black: no need to see beyond
the glass. It shows up next to nothing
when he holds it to the light. Small
wonder that he also relishes the night,
the long walk home without a torch,
his house, unlit, beside the woods.

You cannae fear what you cannae see.

Tonight, the last one in the bar, he gives
a nod, fumbles for his coat, winds his scarf
as tight as he can bear it round his throat.
Be seeing you again. Across the pub, in turn,
those other, silent drinkers set their glasses
down, follow him onto the country lane
that leads away from town.

a mild for stainless stephen

He haunts the chippies mostly,
nodding his approval
at the puns: *Posh Plaice,*
A Salt & Battery, In Cod We Trust.

Dressed up to the nines
in stainless shoes, a plated vest,
two spoons for a bow tie, a fork
to comb his sleek, black hair

he says: *I'm aimless comma*
brainless comma Stainless Stephen
semi-colon semi-conscious
ordering my chips full stop.

And when the shop lads
shove him out into the cold,
he knows a pub across the river
where the doors will never shut,

a shell between the empty works,
where brambles twine around the pumps
and every glass is laced
with spider webs. Where men stride in

still sweating from the braziers
that vanished thirty years ago
and tug their collars,
loosening the noose of heat.

The jukebox hasn't changed its tune
since '71. The landlord stands,
a statue at the bar, as Stainless
saunters in and tips his silver hat,

surveys his audience –
the roughed up chairs, the yawning
window panes, the shabby walls
that echo back his jokes

as if they know each one by heart.
Semi-quaver, semi-frantic,
Stainless croons the golden oldies,
sing-alongs to sway to,

here in Sheffield
where they drink till dawn
and beg for encores, understand
there's no such thing as *Time*.

a vodka for the working ghosts

Have pity, then, on long-dead steelworkers,
whose curse confines them to the northern quarters –
Kelham Island, Meadowhall: the land

encircled by a leat, shops built
where furnaces once breathed.
On Friday nights they loiter by the pubs,

or pace beside the working girls
who don't look up, move through the shadows
lithe as water from the Don.

On Saturdays they glide between
fractious shoppers, press their noses
to the glass facade of Debenhams,

observe the plastic salad tossers, nylon sweaters,
can-can rows of disembodied legs displaying
fashion tights. They'll stare at what they cannot touch

for evermore, at home and helpless in this town
that takes its name from *Sheaf*, from separation,
famed for its production of knives.

a shot for the ghost in the x-ray machine

The ancient nurse who haunts the Derby Royal
        x-ray booth is nothing
if she's not a slave to truth: beneath the blueprints
        of our bones,
her scans reveal those secrets we thought
        safe until the grave.

On Ward 15, a woman strokes her husband's hand,
        or gently
smoothes her straw-blonde hair, for who
        is she to guess
as she reclines against her chair, that soon
        the nurse will call her in

and trace the outline of her ribcage, then,
        below its latticework, the silver
calligraphy of her lover's name
        etched on a pocket watch
she gave to him three years ago?

And if her doting husband were to break his leg
        one day, in some small mishap
on the rain-slicked, flagstone patio, the scans would show
        his femur hides the slender penknife

he once held against a woman's throat, half-cut
        on brandy, joking
that his hand might slip, while she stood trembling
        against the wall.
Don't panic, love. It were a joke. I've had a few,
        that's all.

short measure for the gabriel hound

Each time I read a cloud's dark countenance
or watch two crows stitch out a warning
in the clear blue air, I can't forget

the Bradwell miners, bound for home
without a lamp to guide them, night as heavy
as the earth they'd toiled beneath all day.

They heard the long grass stir. They stood
stock still. A beam, sharp as a skinning knife
shone from the moon down to the hill and carved

the huge shape of a hound: a dog so quick
they'd barely taken flight before they heard it bay
and felt its harsh breath at their heels. They ran

full speed with burning lungs until the dawn,
until the daylight overtook them and they went,
grim-faced, down to the mine

to meet their certain fate. Remember them
as you lie in bed, when the empty house
has fallen still, and you stare through open curtains

at a starless sky, imagine it's a dog's
black flank that passes you, bound
for somewhere else tonight.

a mixer for the hitchhiker

Past midnight on the road to Owler Bar,
I tell myself the story of the pale-faced hitch-hiker
who waited here for headlights in the thicket-dark.

In some accounts the evening's still and moonless.
In other tales, the sky is punched with stars so bright
the lorry driver sees him in their downy light.

But no-one doubts the detail of his deadly silence
as they drove, those flint-blue eyes that never lifted
from the road ahead, no matter what was said to him,

or how, just shy of town, the driver glanced across
and found the seat was empty,
the dark outside was silent as his own dark grave:

its carved inscription suddenly seen clear
as if he stood before it in the churchyard, looking down,
and knew the very air was rid of him.

a ghost in my house

'I Dwell in a lonely house I know
That vanished many a summer ago,
And left no trace but the cellar walls,
And a cellar in which the daylight falls,
And the purple-stemmed wild raspberries grow'.

Robert Frost

a chaser for miss heath

At seventy, our dance mistress
could still perform
a perfect *pas des chats.*

Her French was wasted
in the north. We stood in line
repeating *parr-durr-shat*

or sniggered
as she waited in the wings,
her right hand beating time

against her hip, her eyes
avoiding ours. She never
made the stage.

It took me twenty years
to understand. Alone tonight
and far from home

in shoes that pinch my toes
until they bleed, my back
held ballerina straight,

I wait as she did, too afraid
to walk into a bar
where everyone's a stranger.

I almost see her glide
across the city night
to meet me, tall and white

and slim. A step behind,
she clicks her fingers. Elegant,
she counts me in.

a single for the double

Who was it walked beside me
from the lintel of The Anchor, out
across four unlit fields to home?

He smelled of Hamlet smoke
and mothballs; grandad's overcoat
that smothered me when I was small

and through his whisky breath
he whistled sea shanties, the lullabies
my mother never sang. His steps

were softer than my own, like one
who'd hesitate before a door
afraid to knock, and in the dark,

I almost took his hand to pull him
close, then checked myself, remembered
poor Professor Parkins and his fiend,

the whistle that he called it with
imagining no harm could come to him
across the shingled beach. I drew away

and when, at last, we reached
the five bar gate that marks the first house
of the lane, I bit my lip and turned,

prepared to face his shape gone slinking
through the stubble field, or waiting
in the shelter of the hedge.

I was alone. The wind fell still.
I stood to watch as one by one, the yellow
eyes of every house in town blinked shut.

14

a dram for all the men i've never drunk with

Sigmund Freud refuses every neat Ardbeg
or soft Caol Isla swirled beneath his nose

but Byron knocks them back in one, then winks
and taps his glass against the lacquered tabletop.

Beside me, Marx is dishing out full measures
of the sherry-finished, twelve-year old Ledaig

but Larkin's nothing but a bitter man, he says,
he'll have no truck with spirits.

I've brought them to my local, in the snug
armpit of Sheffield, where the landlord

doesn't bat an eyelid if my wise companions
sometimes slip their guard;

pass fingers through their glasses, take a shortcut
through a wall to reach the loos. *It's Sat'dy neet*

he says, *there's stranger folk in here than these*.
And, after all, he's seen the likes of me before as well;

he gently lifts us out of corner seats
past closing time, the women who arrive alone,

who murmur toasts into the air, who raise a glass
to men who've never answered them.

a gin for spring

To bring your laughter back,
I exorcised the house. First, the kitchen
where last night some poltergeist
had flung your willow-pattern plates
against the wall, and split the white skull
of the fruitbowl.

In the lounge, I stoppered
dark green bottles, corked whatever
spirits slipped from them,
invoked the chanting of the radio,
the incantation of the football scores
against whatever lingered here.

I held your silver pendant aloft
as if it were a charm and placed
a talisman of daffodils in every room.
Upstairs, I shook your white bedsheets
until whatever had you weeping in the night
was loosed into the April air.

When the house was clean
I turned to look at all I'd done, realised
what I'd missed: you were still standing
in the garden, staring past the snowdrops
at the dark hedgerow behind. In the face of spring,
you saw the bones of winter.

a pint for dad

You say you've never seen a Brocken Spectre
haunt the ragged Scottish hills behind you,
never turned your head as you climbed alone

and seen your likeness in the mist, a silent figure
drawing close. No double, tracking you up Blaven
and Sgurr Alasdair, the countless lonely peaks you loved.

But now the English doctors talk of murmurs
in your heartbeat: irregularity, an echo
just as if a second pulse were hammering in your veins.

Dad, if you can't run beside me anymore,
keep pace with me up Kinder Scout, Win Hill,
Black Rocks, if you can't climb the pockmarked face

of grey Mam Tor, think of me as your Brocken Spectre.
Know that as the blizzards lash the tops
I'll still be out there: gaining height,

I'm running up the frown-lines of the hill,
keeping to a track you pointed out for me
ten years ago.

full measure for neil moss

Who spoke it first, the old lie
that the dead don't answer back?
Each time I step over a storm drain
or a crack, I hear him call:
the Oxford caver who they lost
in '59 and couldn't reach, down
in the fissured depths of Castleton
though, searching in the dark
they heard his cries
as clear as he heard theirs.

From gaps and passageways,
I hear him call to me,
the way, some nights, we swear
we hear our own names spoken
though there's no-one there
and turn in quiet avenues
or terraces to nothing
but the ululation of the wind,
the thin soprano of a cat
at someone else's door.

What peace for those
who wait unreached, below
the ground? Their voices seep
into our guarded light;
through late-night cafe chains
and spot-lit bars, through all
the bright places we go
to shake them off, drain
our glasses dry, pretend
we're deaf to them. Tonight,

from Castleton, from Carsington
they call to us, from reservoirs
and mine shafts, long since shut,
from bricked-up wells and tunnel mouths.
Tonight, they cast their voices out
like pit canaries, certain
that this time the sound
will be returned, certain
that it won't be long
till we come back to them.

last orders for chesterfield

So homesick in the fens
I couldn't sleep, I rose before
this morning's dawn

and groped downstairs
to find a rusty bicycle
abandoned at my gate.

I rode due north until
I reached the town I left behind
two years ago. Here,

it is spring and all the streets
are emptying their pockets
to the early breeze:

the air alive with starlings,
scraps of newspaper, laughter
of night-shift workers going home.

I scan the bus stop for a face
I recognise, though nobody
will meet my stare. And then I see

the churchyard wall is clean
of my dark signature. The pubs
have changed their names.

The Rec is wrapped
in an amnesia of hawthorn bushes,
russet skeletons of cars.

Behind the stripped out cinema
the buses glide straight past me
as I try to flag them down

and beside the taxi rank,
the waiting drivers don't look up
or step aside to let me pass,

animated by a story
one of them's rehearsed all night;
the lass he rescued out at B'oser

picked her up without
a scrap of clothing on. *Lover's tiff,*
he says, *the slapper was locked out.*

And as I walk unrecognised
up Hady Hill, and check
the houses for the comfort

of my own reflected face,
the night is catching up with me.
I can't stop picturing

a girl alone and naked,
shivering on the wrong side
of the windowpane

and further from that world
than if she were a thousand
miles away. And I know

even before I've passed
the butcher's shop, the corner store,
the park's black railings,

slick as spears, I know
that when I reach my parents' house
it will be overgrown

with waist high-nettles, choked
by ivy, hidden by thorns.
I know before I've even

reached my local, with its
saloon doors that never closed
to anyone, I know

that I could stand here at the bar
for hours, because the landlord
will not see me,

though he might pause to wonder
what it is that seems to stir
there in the tap room

as he switches all the lights off
and brings the boards in,
then stands in the beer garden

dragging on his cigarette,
staring at the moon, which
on a night like this, almost seems

to smoke in the dark above him;
a gun barrel after the last shot
has been fired.

afterword

after hours

I belong
to starless nights:
the six black boulders
up at Harthill moor who dance
like women till the cockerel crows
and morning freezes them again.

I belong
on lonely mountain roads
or underneath the bridges
of canals where coachmen
whip their ghostly horses,
ships pass through dry land.

I belong
with phantom Lancasters
that light the evening sky
like fireflies above Kinder,
or seem to crash
into the headstone of the hill.

I belong
in long-deserted pubs
with the tap room poltergeist,
the Irish prize-fighter, who still
has scraps to start, who swings
at late-night drinkers

with his fists of air
and won't be carried out.

a mild for stainless stephen

Arthur Clifford Baynes (1892–1971) was a comedian from Sheffield who performed under the stage name Stainless Stephen. He would appear dressed in a tuxedo, a rotating bow tie, and a stainless steel vest. His trademark was his peculiar intoned monologues. He never achieved enough fame to allow him to give up his day job as an English teacher.

a shot for the ghost in the x-ray machine

In January 2009, Derby City General Hospital called in a priest to exorcise one of its x-ray machines after multiple sightings of a cloaked figure, dressed in black.

short measure for the gabriel hound

In English folklore, 'Gabriel Hound' refers to a mysterious creature, often a huge dog, whose howls signify an ill omen. However, this poem bases its narrative more closely on the story of two young miners at Bradwell, who were making their way home when they encountered a strange animal, believed to be an omen of death in the pit.

a single for the double

Professor Parkins is the unfortunate protagonist in M.R. James' famous story 'Oh, Whistle, and I'll Come to you, My Lad', pursued by a fiend he has unwittingly summoned.

a pint for dad

A Brocken Spectre is an optical illusion sometimes seen in the hills: the magnified shadow of an observer, cast upon the upper surfaces of clouds. The head of the figure is often surrounded by glowing halo-like rings.

full measure for neil moss

On March 22nd, 1959, Neil Moss, a student at Balliol College Oxford, was part of an expedition to explore a newly discovered fissure in Peak Cavern near Castleton (known as 'The Devil's Arse'). Moss became jammed after descending a narrow shaft and attempts to rescue him failed. He died on March 24th, and his body was never recovered. This section of Peak Cavern is now known as Moss Chamber.